Beady Eyed & Mystified

by

Maclean Mbepula

Beady Eyed & Mystified

Copyright © 2019 Maclean Mbepula
www.CreativeAfrica.Space
info@creativeafrica.space

All rights reserved.

Dedication

For Patrick, Martha and Sarah:
loved and forever missed.

… and those who marvel at the
world; beady-eyed and mystified.

Contents

Acknowledgments

I would like to thank **everyone** who helped make this book possible: those who helped me make up my mind when it was indecisive, those who gave my life content and those who helped me live it. Thanks also go to the audiences that made me feel understood as I performed some of what's in this book and convinced me by their support that something like this was worth writing.

A special thanks to those of my artist friends that reviewed and critiqued this work as this book was shaped. Thanks to Lilongwe's Living-room Poetry Club for the platform to share my work. Lastly but not least, thanks to God for all this. To all of you and anyone I forgot: thank you.

1. Art & Things

"Its life on these pages
Is its death in me?"

I Guess

I guess it's good that you broke me
I guess it's good that you tore me apart
because when you did,
And I became undone,
All these words fell out.
And then I called it poetry

So, I guess
this
is

ok.

Write it Out

If it could be cut out with a carving knife,
I would
I would take the knife and cut it right out of me
But I can't.
I can only write it out,
Describe it into this world of man
and hope
and only hope that its spirit is birthed on these pages
So I don't have to think about it anymore
And that its life on these pages
Is its death in me
I am tired of this wretched companion
Whose only words are those I've heard before
Telling me everything with grandiose emotion that only wound me further
still.
That only repeat to me
Matters of my very inadequacies which are plain as day
already
And make me want to fetal position myself into oblivion.
If that was even possible.

2. The Self

*"We are the emotional equivalents of 5 year olds
left in a room with breakable things"*

I Say Again

You are stardust,
I say again, you are stardust!
May you be sprinkled everywhere,
so that when the light touches you,
the world -
It shines!
Because
of you.

Uncreated Words

There is no word created
No phrase designed
That can help me explain to you what I think you can't grasp
Hey, I am more than you see
This chapter you walked in on, is incomplete -
This, is NOT ME!
Or at least it's not me in my entirety.
You acknowledge and respect the differences
But you refuse to acknowledge and respect that I am a puzzle missing many
of its pieces.
And by the way: so are you.
See, I know there is absolutely no way that you can understand that
I know there is no language, dialect, cultural persuasion, or even universe
that exists where what I say will make sense to you
Because your head understands, hears and chooses only to believe your
voice -
Your words, your decision at your time and in your way.
So these words I speak are uncreated
'Unmeaningful'
Non-existent
Virtually Nothing
Less than Empty
To you

Messy

Some of us are messy
We are the emotional equivalents of 5-year-olds left in a room with breakable things
Unchaperoned, excited, driven delirious by all the new and shiny things around us
We touch,
We toy,
We break it!
And then we cry Justin Timberlake the rivers he asked for
Because that's what we do
We are afraid
But we are hopeful
...But we are alone,
trying to understand everything that we are supposed to know
Gravitating towards things that sparkle and glisten in the light
Whether they are soft and squishy
Or cold, metallic, pointy and sharp
We just think if we get close to that, we'll understand it and love it
It still hasn't yet sunk in that fire burns, even right to the bone
… and not even right to the bone… but right to the soul
It hasn't yet stuck that pointy things are sharp and can cut and bruise
Cutting right through where the heart and mind meet
leaving you torn apart…
Even though it's happened before.

Feels

There are exactly 1592 different types of "feels".
A true feeler would know
There isn't just anger, jealousy, love, hope, fear
hate, despair…
Oh, there is so much more!
These 1592 different "feels" aren't just degrees of hate, or love or hope or what have you.
They are each unique…
and only something someone in tune with their feels can understand.
Only they can understand how you can be happy and sad all at the same time.
Only they can tell you how you can feel content and discontent all in the while
Only they know the torment and joy of having the super human ability of feeling everything all at once.
All 1592 different feels.

Fight, Flight, Calm

Capture yourself, capture yourself,
As you start to flee
Third eye, look, this is me!

Hold yourself, hold yourself
As you start to fight
Restraint, restraint, hold me with all your might

Picture yourself, picture yourself
Transformed through the dark of night
Remember, remember, you can be alright

3. Relationships

"Tell me you counted every second
that was meant for me"

Listen

No judge, no jury, no shooting squad needed.
Just someone like me to listen
Them two ears turned in my direction
and that bleeding heart you've got, bleeding for me just that one second or
two
No judgment. No solution. No fixing, No illusions.
None, just listen.
No flattery. No painting over.
No anecdotes. No prescriptions. No flipping "Now, you see your problem
here is..."
No, just listen, today.
No brainstorming. No guardian-angelesque escapading. No riding or
dying just right now.
Just be human. Just right now...
Just sit and just listen.
Today.
Tomorrow, perhaps, I'll ask for advice on this here matter
but today,
Just listen.

Where Were You?

Tell me you went to climb the Alps for the past 10 months straight -
That would be understandable.
Tell me you fell down a flight of stairs,
Got rushed to the hospital and was found with a malignant ailment that
rendered you out of circulation for the better part of this year.
Tell me you had a spiritual awakening and abandoned social media in the
hope of becoming a better person, and paid someone else to post on your
behalf to keep up with appearances
Say you thought of me from time to time and pined over us
Tell me nothing tasted the same.. just "cardboardy" without me
Tell me you spent your waking moments wondering what was missing
and every time your thoughts freely floated towards thoughts of me
Tell me you dreamed of me
And every night you would rehearse an apology
Tell me a thousand nights you tried and couldn't get passed, "I'm sorry"
Tell me you stored every hug you owe me
And you counted every second that was meant for me
Say you noted it down for my recompense.
Abandon believability
Like you abandoned me
I am naive enough to believe anything you say if it sounds sincere enough
I don't need "plausible"
I just need hope.
A little bit.
Tell me you are the person I thought I had always known.
Because at least if I don't know where you've been
I can try and be content with who you are.

A Thousand Times

You killed me a thousand times with a single blow
And every time I resurrected, I died once more
The pain; you couldn't believe.
Until I drew a sword and for a second watched you bleed
I am sorry
because I know:
I did that.

I held a hand to hurt you
I struck you with such hope
Not to hurt you for harms sake
But that somehow I could make you feel for a second, just a second,
One of the deaths you dealt me
Somehow with my mind warped with deep emotion, that made sense at the
time
As I did now, all you would see is
My dagger drawn when yours was not raised this time

I'm sorry.

Maclean T. Mbepula

Shell

I find myself withdrawing -
into a shell I didn't know I had,
Finding solace in the thought that
Maybe from here,
You can't hurt me
Because now you can't reach me
Yet I find myself wondering what I'm missing
But every thought is tinged with the flavor of experience
Reminding me that no matter what I miss
I am safer here
Hidden,
In my shell
I fear this will harden my soul and heart
Until they are calcified
in that leprosy-type way
But somehow
That's okay
Because you can't hurt me here.

Old Fashioned

I prefer a postal letter
Because then we put more thought into the message that's sent
Now we are flippant
Rash,…
Making sentences from words which we sometimes only half know the
meaning of
If I could
I would
Kamikaze my digital presence and leave you with my postal address
So only the most sincerest messages are sent and received
My old soul longs for words that matter
And not just those sent in convenience
And habit

Those of us

Those of us who are unforgettable get upset when we are forgotten
Those of us who are memorable get surprised when we are ill-remembered
Those of us who are lovable get sad when we are unloved
Those of us who are towering infernos get chilled to the bone when our flames are left alone
Those of us who hearken these storms get riveted when the tides turn those of us...

In the Kingdoms

In the kingdoms where I'm from
There where many kings and queens
Who each had land to rule.
I , to watch over them all.

An enemy came
Who had never known defeat but once.
He attacked with the darkest of armies, our weakest of lands.
When called to arms,
Some of these honoured kings and queens ignored our call
There would be blood shed, they knew.

but this, was not their battle
This was not their war.

Some came even from far away across the seas
To fight with us, against this
Prince of thieves.

Side by side, ironically battling to claim back our peace.
How they could behave as kin before our own?
Our hearts could never come to know.

Sure enough as time would show,

We had come to vanquish our foe
And those who failed us in our darkest hour,
Our hearts did not have the power

To make believe that their swords had been drawn with us in epic strife.
We did not have the depth of imagination to pretend that they had gone
with us.

Slain with us
Died as some of us
And resurrected with us on the battle field

Now with the semblance of peace that one can only know once a battle's
done, these charading kings and queens, they did come.

With jubilant praise
With jovial gaits of which you approach your long lost, with their crooked
arms open wide to embrace us

We told them, "We do not know you.
Our blood was shed on that field you refused to go. We do not know you.
You, are not our own."

That is how we dethroned them all.
That is how we raised some kingdoms from across the shores.
Our kings and queens are those that raise their swords with us,
That held their shields for us,
That side by side, they are with us.
These are of us, these we know.
These, indeed, are our own.

4. Anxiety, Pain and Depression

"And since you don't fight the sea - you flow.
what are you to do?"

Secret Message

I have come with a secret message
They are coming to get you.
They said they are going to bury you
Marry you to the soil
Place you – six feet deep
and your body will be buried under a soily heap

I have come to warn you
that time is running out
Make your way out and let them not find you here
Pack your bags and let them see that you are
No longer here...

when they come

Of the Sea

I found myself swept in a sea
One hundred feet from shore
I hadn't noticed the waves had carried me, or would carry me more
When I awoke to the faint whisper of a shout
Or a shout of a whisper - about
My drift :
I heard, "Don't go"
And since you don't fight the sea - you flow
What are you to do?
No paddle to row
No anchor to undraw
No fibre of flesh to restrain
Nothing but sea
Nothing to see but conniving water droplets holding hands and planning a
secret path to wherever they want,
Where ever they want me to go.

5. Humour

*Definitely *not* as funny
as I initially thought.*

Shipwrecked black woman

One beautiful sunny day,
my friends and I decided to sail away in the big blue sea
See, one of my buddies was very monied
and had a family boat sitting pretty, in the bay by the beach
So, we sailed off a bit to enjoy life, philosophize and forget the busy-nesses
and stresses.
Three days we said, to relax and clear our heads.
But my friend, the yacht owner, was a novice at sailing, soon we learned,
and one thing led to another, and we got swept off course
Then the weather changed into a furious storm
and we all started to long for our respective norms

I can't remember what happened next until the point where I woke up
in the warm seas with my friends crying out, trying to find me
I'd been floating precariously on our giant cooler box and managed to pass
out and
well my friends too were bobbing up and down in the gentle waves
and the luxury yacht my friend owned wasn't anywhere to be seen except for a
few bits and bobs.

"Well, I suppose that is that"
People will try and find us eventually, we rationalized
as we swam to the shore that appeared somewhere yonder before our eyes
And yes, they'll search for us and we'ld be rescued in no time.

But no time, was a long time
No one came for us and we started to lose hope.
The drinks in the cooler ran out by day 4, even though we tried to ration
them.
None of us had bothered to Youtube things like
"How to make a spear for fishing?"

"How to fish with your bare hands"
Or how to locate fresh water like the Koi Koi.
Finally we picked some coconuts...
We had one week straight of coconut!!

There's only so much coconut that people can eat

And you could see in their eyes -
their bodies needed some meat
No wild bores or anything to hunt
and my friends weren't really alpha males,
they were at their physical best competing in some computer hackathon.

I being the more ample of three
well, let's just say my number was up
and dinner, would be me!

This body

This body
has been loved
by every potato chip
And every fried sausage,
By every ice-cream cone
and every grilled cheese sandwich
dripping,
Simply dripping, with its steamy juice

This body
has been
caressed
Sublimely caressed, by one to four
Kit-Kat fingers at a time.
Gently frolicking and melting in my mouth
That cocoa driving me insane!

This body has known seduction
Seduction at its ultimate core.
arresting and binding
When that pizza calls out my name!
Gently calling my name!
These nostrils have known the sweet scent of syrups
custards and nectar
as it drips on mountains of smooth, delectable pancakes
or cake or ice-cream

Sweet nothings have been whispered over and over again
in an infinite lie of eternity, yet so brief
with only the scale and the dentist to taint it.
To taint, what this body has known.

6. Tragedy & Loss

*"They came to be in my sphere of being
but they weren't mine.*

Not one day"

It's Funny Now

She told me how
her finger nails and hair had fallen off
And somehow we found a joke in there, somewhere.
We laughed:
She laughed
I did too
I suppose it was a big "screw you"!
to the terror that stood
And made me cry at night
the terror that changed our lives
and finally took her away
At least we found a way to mock it
So that that terror
was now
the butt of a joke
that only us two could understand
But even so,
before that terror got the better of us,
For a brief moment
of which in another universe -
it could have been an eternity
- for that brief moment:
the terror was stupid
impotent
and
inconsequential
Nothing
to
fear.
In
that joke,
she said
"It's funny Now."

Cherry Tomatoes

They trampled over them in their efforts to clear nature's carnage
I had been looking forward to seeing these cherry tomatoes turn bright red
from their green hue
I'ld inspect them from time to time with on almost OCD-level interest
Just kind of hoping to see one be the first to ripen and redden
It didn't happen
They trampled over those cherry tomatoes
And they were gone
I didn't know they had been loaned to me for just a look and no taste
Kind of felt upset thinking, they had been robbed from me
But the truth is: they had never been mine
They came to be in my sphere of being but they weren't mine
Not one day,
More over I didn't farm them into that spot…

7. Death / Grief

"A thousand nerves awake all at once
Feeling it all, feeling it all, feelings real raw"

It Felt Like

Someone just pressed play on the video,
Yet there was no sound
It felt like there
should be sunlight but there's only darkness around
It felt like a thousand nerves awake all at once
Feeling it all, feeling it all, feelings real raw,

It felt like a
day I could never have planned
Surreal, but real but surreal
A thousand feels
and yet it felt like I

was dead to the sense
I heard the words but my matter was dense
This is a, this is b
This is the total to those cents
But how could this happen
when you promised defense?

It felt like a lie.

8. God & Spirituality

*"If you listen hard you will hear the echo of my voice
in the girth of His laughter"*

Evolution Illusion Theory

The story of my life is written in his smile lines,
a crystal clear image of me is reflected in His eyes
and if you listen hard you will hear the echo of my voice in the girth of His
laughter.
How could I simply have evolved from gaseous happenings of non-causical
chance?
How could it be that I am anything less than the musings of a mastermind
gone wild on his palette of life and creation?
Like a painter,
furiously making stroke after stroke after stroke after stroke after stroke
until
he stood aback and knowing in the completest of knowingness said, "It is
finished"
and it was done.

He was done.

I was done in Him.

I think this is what God says:

You're naked,
butt naked!!!
let me clothe you
You are stupid
Incredibly stupid
let me give you content for your thoughts
You're lost
Use me as your destination, path and sign post
You're afraid
Hide in me.
Just hide in me
Just hiiiiide in me!
No one can find you here
And no one could ever hurt you here
You are heavy in sin
Where's the hose pipe?
I'll wash it all off you
and dry you in my wings
I want you here,
next to me
Hear me breath
(Smells like mint right?)
Get close enough to hear me breath
I want you here!

9. Surreal – Other Worldly

"Where the stars shine
even in the noon day"

Galaxy

Somewhere across the galaxy,
There's a place where the stars shine even in the noon day
There's a sunshine that feeds your soul
and an echo of forever
that doesn't feel unwelcome
You can taste joy with your tongue
There
You can hear another's heart beat
even with your ears shut
And in this place
The rainbow comes before the rain
Just to remind you that
rain isn't an end in herself
It's weird I know
Perhaps folly to believe
that such a place can be conceived in the same reality that we live in
But who is to say, it doesn't?

10. Malawi & Africa

'I'm not sure I know what a calabash is…"

My African Poem

I'm not sure I know what a calabash is
I must have looked it up once when I read
'When Things Fall Part' …or other
However, I have many poems
and not one mentions
calabashes
not one mentions misty mornings where my bare feet traversed the dry
African plains
not one about a hyena, or a snake or a lion or an elephant
though I do love elephants,
They are such compassionate creatures,
Even more so than some human beings have the capacity to ever be
And I am beginning to wonder if my story is at all
authentic
If I am at all worthy to be African
I've taken or borrowed all my *chitenjes* from my mother and cousin
three in total
Never bought one!
and I own possibly two items of clothing in African print
This is authentically me
but I wonder if it is enough culture to be deemed
African.

The Africa that I know

The Africa that I know,
She stands with pride and walks with flow
When she speaks, her sound forces mountains to turn and peer
And with her voice, she's sincere
Says, "You are princes and princesses, kings and queens – my dears,
That is your heritage, no matter what it seems."
She doesn't know it but, she's selling us dreams – everyday
And we, we keep buying and buying, anyway.

Maybe confused by her beauty: with greens, reds, yellows, blues
of all hues and browns like that of clay
We see, but we don't see all the way
Does she block our view
Since she's larger than life, bursting at the seams with variety?
Seemingly always with some potential of enormous virility
If I know, anything,
I know this
Good or bad, she's a show off,
She truly is

The Africa that I know,
You fall in love with - even if your straight
Her soul is her bait
Now, the thing is, she's not lying
Sometimes, maybe she's trying
She means it, when she says to you and me
"You can be all that you want to be"

It's just that some learned this sooner
And took all the shiny stuff that makes dreams come true
So now, there's not enough for me and definitely not enough for you.
See, the pie they cut,
The left us all with crumbs
In feeble protest, we spoke up but it meant none,
They might as well be deaf and we might as well be dumb.
In all her showing off,
There's little substance – just froth
Yet to her, my thoughts sometimes go

Enchantments aside, I feel sorry for her though
It's like she's this tired woman, who sits,
On a damp floor, in a dingy cell somewhere
Leaning , forlorn, against a grungy wall
With crusty, dirty hair

In worn out and torn clothes
Thrown dry moldy bread from dry moldy loaves
- Once a day, by her captors.
Her captors who turn out to be one of her own sons and one of her own
daughters.
This captive, sent mad by her tragedy,
All she can do is recite her pockets of memory
Memories since faded but for the bits that mattered most
Reminded every time she gazes upon her host.
She mumbles, "You can be all that you want to be".

And out beyond her cell
most not so well
Are the rest of her kin
Those doing great know she's alive and what state she's in.
Those far outside, are oblivious to her plight

Or perhaps knowing but pretending that everything's alright
Mastered by their kin
Who have schemed and plundered and kept their mother hidden in
Sullied by the blood of the evil of their sin
Those outside, comforted only by the faint memory of what she said:
"You are princes and princesses, kings and queens – my dears,
    That is your heritage, no matter what it seems. "

Neo-slave Freedom Song

Empty pockets, no dough
but we're coming

dirty hands,
one hoe
but we're coming

bare feet
lean meat,
but we're coming

held back,
no more
 coz we're coming

Heard that?!
Quote us,
coz we're coming!

11. Society

"Of worms and butterflies"

Maclean T. Mbepula

The Master

What the master called a butterfly
the world called a flying worm
What the painter called a flower
the world called weed and thorn

They Don't Know

Disheveled
Ugly
Unembraceable
Unpresentable

They didn't know he had just won a battle

Torn clothes
stains
that looked like dry blood
or mud

They didn't know he had just come out alive

Slow steps
Weary but steady gait
bruises on his cheek
puffed out chest but
air of the meek

That look of experience that one look can tell
That look that says, " I've just been to hell"

They didn't know

he had just finished the war

I Caught a Star

I caught a star as it whizzed by
It was going so fast and so far
But I caught a star
It tingled as I felt it
It shimmered as I held it
hands now blooded & charred from catching a shooting star
But there was nothing I felt
except to appreciate the fact
that I caught a star

All I could think of was
"Quick, I must show another"

So I thought to show it to someone else
I was mesmerized
This star was my golden prize
So, I like a child, holding it & beady eyed
I went in haste to share
to anyone who would listen, anyone who was there.

This star, it dazzled me,
It filled me with delight
and wonder.

I took it to a neighbour and they said
it was a rock
It was rock and dust,
Nothing more
Please kindly get out my door
I was outraged and I said
Can't you see?
Are you blind
This is a star - a shining prize,
Please just open your eyes
I caught it last night
This could be cryptonite!

Encouraged to leave, I gently walked away
I'll never forget that lonely ineffectual day

And again, the next person said the same.
Oh, the shame.
But If I hadn't seen it whizzing past with my own eyes, I too would think
the same.

So now I just stand in a tiny corner of a dusty busy street
Hoping to share with whomever I meet
About my prize, my star
Sometimes I wonder: should I have let it go on its way?
Should I have not caught it and made it stay?
But, would I have known then,
that it's possible for the child of men
to catch a shooting star.
...when it's going so fast, and so far.

Never

Never hold people down
Who are meant to fly
Because one day
One day the fire in their bellies
Will set them aflame
And this fire will burn you alive
It will break the chains that are your hands
And they will soar
Phoenix-wise
And they will survey the plains you stopped them from seeing
From knowing.
And yours
Yours, which would have been a beautiful legacy
Will be the pitiful story of one caught on the wrong side of history
Not even God stops one from flying
Who are you to try?
Never.
Stop.
Another's
Flight.

12. Life Matters

"Scrolling, scrolling, scrolling"

Certain

I am certain.
That certainty in itself is uncertain.
I am certain that everyone who thinks they have it all figured out
Have that one question that is thrown at them
that they just can't answer
Oh, the vanity or illusion of certainty
Dressed in earnest vivid presentation
But I bet you
I bet you there's a night sometimes
Where certainty herself stays up
Sat on the side of her bed
wondering about
"What ifs" and "what abouts'
What, wheres and maybe, maybe even a doubt
she entertains
I am pretty certain,
That certainty laughs loud at our certainty
Certain that certainty maybe even a figment of her own imagination
Maybe she doesn't exist
Maybe she does
Maybe she does and doesn't from time to time.
… which in itself is an impossibility
- but are you certain?
Certainly, there is that.

Scrolling

I scrolled as though something in me was searching for something specific
on the page
Subconsciously scanning, skimming and reading,
Liking, sharing and thinking…
Restless because whatever my inner me was looking for
Wasn't there
And I know that the next time I scroll
I still won't find it
Whatever "it" is.

It's a Process – Keep Going

Fickle
Untethered
Unhinged
Life is many, many things.
It's everything you want or don't want it to be
With able body or not
Life implores you to get up and get going
Life is like cold water thrown in your face on a cold and frosty day
Life is like a cool breeze in the shade in the warm summer heat
but whatever and where it is, life simply says, "keep going".

In the war time or at peace
In love or unrequited
Life is life

With broken bones,
gorged out eyes
with smiles or frowns
with disease or stellar health
With success or in failure
Life is life
And life it says, "keep going"

When your best friend departs the world of the living
When your family dies, one by one...
When you are alone except for yourself,
The emptiness around echoes, "Keep going"

Life it says, "Never stop, never cease...
You must only stop when you arrive where you ought to be
Who, oh who, has ever arrived where they need to go, by standing still
Unless of course, they are already where they must be?

When at last, your race has been lost or won,
Victories fought or shunned,
Breathes inhaled and exhaled
Lives intertwined and released – and intertwined again

When even you yourself, when even you die,
You must do what life has always said
Even in the afterlife -
"Keep going".

The Christmas Tree

There were no Christmas trees to buy that winter
As the road to that part of town was impassable
So, I went into the forest and pulled down something of a branch
Semi-dead… or dead, I don't know…
and I took it like it was the most expensive tree I ever bought
and I put it in the side of the living room… right by the window
… I stood it up in an empty Nido tin can.. that I wrapped in some leftover
purple wrapping paper.
Shiny

I barely put anything on it
But you wouldn't have guessed it
If you saw my face from my window
You wouldn't have guessed
that this naked barely living crooked thing
was better than the most giant of pine trees.
More majestic than a majesty clad in his robe.

I would catch myself smiling from time to time.
Lost in thought of what it meant
stuck in a vision that naked eyes could never see.

13. Milestones & Memories

"Before…
anything was said"

Wasted

I pulled myself out of the dumpster you threw me into
I dusted away all the yuck
All the 50 different types of yuck that stained my
 person
I had words for you
But I have learned
They are better left unsaid.

Before

Before
anyone told me
You get to be just "one thing"
Before I was told, " Money is god, money is king!"

Before
anyone told me that it was "gay" to stop random strangers in the street
and say,"My gosh, you look lovely."
Before anyone told me that people don't do that.

Before
anyone told me
you had to be exclusively in love to say "I love you"
to people whose hearts yours sometimes beat for
though the injustice of holding those words trapped in your mouth
were like a lie
left to run wild out inside.

Before
anyone told me
that you're not allowed to dream this big
or think this wide...
you're not allowed to think
outside of what everyone has constructed as legitimate and attainable
... and expected

Before
anyone told me
that it was not ok
just not ok to be that person
who sees it raining out
and wants to go outside

Before
anyone told me
it wasn't ok to dance to music in its presence or absence

wherever you find yourself
and it finds you
and that groove moves you, in the streets... in the office...
Before
anything was said

Before there was something wrong with being this...
with being me...

Just before that

I
was invincible
Incredibly so
I was bold
and oblivious... and naive
I was recklessly adoring of life
and a hopeless romantic
I was that dewy-eyed romantic that life was made for
I believed everything
and in everything
and I believed that the world was different from this.

I could see beauty in the snout of a pig
I could see the face of God in darn near everything
Before...
that is
Before,

I caught myself torn between before
and this.

14. Overthinking

'Respite please – report!'

And Then

And then, the thought came.
It twirled and wiggled around
It wiggled and giggled aloud
it jiggled and tumbled about
Get out, get out I said!
You thought, get out!

but then,
It teased and taunted me
It hooked and baited me
It knew and rated me
It almost had it's way with me
Verily verily, for a moment one day, in me.
But then it tried again to come to be
It's decisive,
it's made its mind up
- concretely

And then
It squeezed and crushed me
battered and bashed me
this thought
Respite please – report!
But it continued
this thought again....

Oh Mind

Oh mind,
Quiet yourself
Let me find myself a place amidst the thoughts
Where I can sit for a while
move this and that over there so I can sit
on a cloudy seat
Amidst anxiety and weariness
And piles and piles and piles of
Heavy, pointy
recurring
twirling
rotten and fresh
Piercing
intrusive
thoughts
Stinking with the stench of embarrassment
With an air of "it's not over"
Let me rest a while
You are relentless in how you consume me with what my heart is weary
of
re-living every time you introduce a new
thought
You are relentless in how you consume me with what my heart is weary
of
tired from,
Full off.

15. Survival

"Maybe not gallivanting but hopping…"

Unbroken

Really really broken
nothing but pieces of what was
But delusional enough to believe otherwise
Gallivanting now on one foot instead of two
Maybe not gallivanting but hopping…
To and fro
broken vertebrae
Broken phalanges
Broken everything
But not obvious to self
Thinking
believing
in unbrokenness

The Great Beat Down

You catapulted through the air
But you landed on your feet
Broken bones, everywhere
but you're still ready to compete
You drag yourself across the room
You won't give in to defeat
So you ready yourself
in your head – you get the right voices on repeat
You can't dance anymore so you bob your head to the
  beat

16. Women's Issues

"You are 'Viking'"

The Tempest's Rant

It would appear that it is the sole purpose of some people to make you feel
"less than"
So, when they come at you to prove their reason for being,
Just remember
You are a beast
You are "Viking"
You are a tempest in the wind
You have the energy to pull limb from limb
The power to desecrate anything in your wake
But you are better than that.
You could ravage whole nations if you chose
At any given point in time, you could be the human equivalent to a nuclear
power plant gone awry
Any minute.
You are savage – if you let yourself be
You are the hell within you when your hormones rage
You are the terror that keeps children far from the grave yard's edge
But the day you were born,
You chose to be
a lady
And that is why
you
are better than that.

Loud Silenced Words

They said you will never be anything
You'll never amount to much
They said you will Never succeed in great things that your hands touch
They said because you are a woman, what you do will mean nothing
They said if you are to go far, then it's because a man said, "I'm opening the
door for you. Pass. "
That's what they said.

They said because you are a woman, your voice doesn't matter
They said your voice is emotional and therefore irrational
They said your will is whimsical and cannot be trusted
They said you can't fight because you're not as physically strong as any man.
That's what they said.

But when you overcame the first time.
They, didn't say anything immediately.
Maybe it's because they didn't expect you to go against their word.
But again they started to speak, they said what they had said before
They ignored the success and considered it a fluke.
Out of the ordinary, an anomaly, something that shouldn't happen but did.
They said you are foolish to believe that you can be more than what they
see.
That's what they said...

But when you overcame again,
They were repulsed at your unrealistic take on life
Disgusted by your audacity
That you would disregard the order of society and dare to go in front.
Dare stand in the ranks of man.
And so they said what you are used to hearing that your success will come
to a screeching halt.
They said that your success will amount to only something mediocre.
Something that you cannot even point to in the sands of time...
That you would become a joke if you continue...
That's what they said.

But when they saw that you heard them many times over
And didn't listen to them anymore,
When they saw that their words sounded like nothing to you,
Because that part of your head had become numb

because you continued to overcome,
You continued to stand and walk in front
in that land that even the men were scared to,
Then they realize
That what they had said was not true
So they started to say that you were an outstanding person,
And an exception to the rule, that other women could not be or become
like you
That's what they said
They said the likelihood that anyone could be like you was slim because
women where not biologically, religiously, socially or financially inclined to
excel.
That is what they said.

They said, never again. She is an anomaly.
That's what they said
But soon, they began to see, more women,
Like me becoming like you
More women breaking their mold,
Going against their spoken, written and documented word
Then soon the anomaly that they believed was the case
Could not be considered something strange
Because women all over the world finally couldn't hear what they said.
Now I wonder what they say,
Because that part of my brain has become dead,
That part that could comprehend everything that they said.

About the Author

Maclean Mbepula is an artist and tech-entrepreneur based in Lilongwe, the capital city of Malawi. Maclean founded both Shekinah Invest and Afrineur.

Writing, performing poetry / spoken word and stand-up comedy are some of her passions. Recently she has taken up painting as an additional vehicle of self-expression. She tries to blog but is pathetically inconsistent. Maclean is an empath and ENFP (for those that know what that is). Starting at age 13, she's performed in schools, universities, parties, official gatherings, churches and other events. Her biggest audience has been over well over 2000 people. She's performed in various events but of note are: the Human Rights Day event 2014– special guest being the President of Malawi, Tumaini Festivals and Qoncept Creative's first Anne Kansiime comedy show and their Raaid Mussa and Simmi Aref comedy show in Malawi.

To date, she has written close to 400 poems – some of the not half bad ☺ . By the end of 2019, she authored 3 books: Beady-Eyed and Mystified, Challenge Accepted and Flatline...Beep.

She's happy to perform globally and available for bookings (and other inquiries) at mac@creativeafrica.space . Videos of some of her performances are on Youtube (Creative Africa Space - Channel). Videos of her performances, pictures, blogs, poems, electronic press kit etc can be found at www.creativeafrica.space. You can also connect with her on Twitter: @maclean4real – be warned: she doesn't just tweet about poetry or poems there.

Get connected.